Oceans
and Seas

KINGFISHER

Kingfisher Publications Plc
New Penderel House
283–288 High Holborn
London WC1V 7HZ
www.kingfisherpub.com

First published by Kingfisher Publications Plc 2004
2 4 6 8 10 9 7 5 3

2TR/1204/PROSP/RNB(RNB)/140MA/F

A CIP catalogue record for this book is available from the British Library.

ISBN–13: 987 0 7534 0945 9
ISBN–10: 0 7534 0945 3

Senior editor: Carron Brown
Designer: Joanne Brown
Cover designer: Anthony Cutting
Illustrator: Steve Weston
Picture manager: Cee Weston-Baker
Picture researcher: Rachael Swann
DTP co-ordinator: Sarah Pfitzner
Artwork archivists: Wendy Allison, Jenny Lord
Senior production controller: Nancy Roberts

Printed in China

Acknowledgements
The publishers would like to thank the following for permission to reproduce their material. Every care has been taken
to trace copyright holders. However, if there have been unintentional omissions or failure to trace copyright holders,
we apologise and will, if informed, endeavour to make corrections in any future edition.
b = bottom, c = centre, l = left, t = top, r = right

Photographs: cover t Getty Images (Getty); cover b Natural History Picture Agency; 1 Getty; 2–3 Getty; 4–5 Corbis; 6 Getty; 7tr National
Geographic Image Collection (NGIC); 7cl Nature Picture Library; 7br Minden Pictures/Frank Lane Picture Agency; 8–9 Corbis; 9tl Alamy;
9b Corbis; 11b Corbis; 12–13 Getty; 13tl Oxford Scientific Films (OSF); 13cl OSF; 13br Corbis; 14 Press Association, London; 15 Corbis;
15t Corbis; 16–17 Getty; 16b Science Photo Library (SPL); 17t OSF; 18–19 Ardea; 19tl NGIC; 19br Ardea; 20 Getty; 21 Getty; 21b Nature
Picture Library 22–23 Corbis; 22bl Corbis; 23tl Getty; 24–25 NGIC; 26bl Nature Picture Library; 27tl Nature Picture Library; 27cr Nature
Picture Library; 27b Nature Picture Library; 28–29 Corbis; 28bl Getty; 30b Getty; 31 Ardea; 31bl Ardea; 32bl Corbis; 33t Minden
Pictures/Frank Lane Picture Agency; 33b Image Quest 3D; 34–35 Getty; 34bl Image Quest 3D; 35tl Nature Picture Library; 36–37 Corbis;
36bl SPL; 37tr SPL; 38 Corbis; 39 Getty; 40bl Getty; 40–41 Getty; 41t Getty; 48 Minden Pictures/Frank Lane Picture Agency.

Commissioned photography on pages 42–47 by Andy Crawford
Project-maker and photoshoot co-ordinator: Miranda Kennedy
Thank you to models Lewis Manu and Rebecca Roper

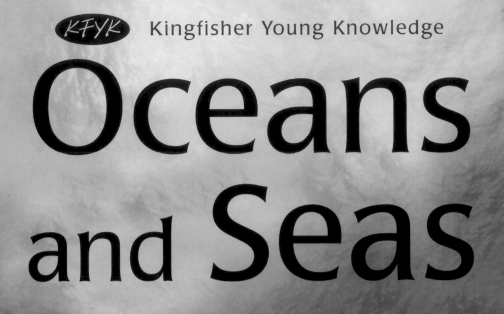

KFYK Kingfisher Young Knowledge

Oceans and Seas

Nicola Davies

Contents

Planet ocean

Only one-third of the earth is dry land, so our planet looks blue when seen from space. The rest of the planet is ocean, and there is life in every part of it!

an ocean is a large sea

Sunlit surface

The ocean's surface is full of tiny plants and animals called plankton, which bigger creatures, such as these jellyfish, eat.

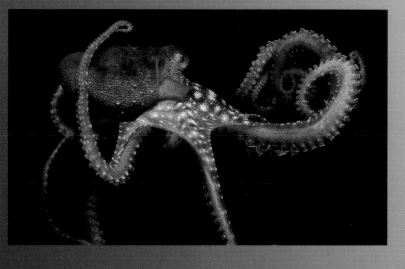

Keeping hidden

Many animals, like this octopus, prefer the deeper water of the middle ocean. Here they can hide from predators and be safe from storms.

Deep and dark

The deepest waters are totally dark and cold. Food is hard to find, so animals here have big mouths, to eat anything!

predators – *animals that hunt and eat other animals*

Salty sea

All seas and oceans are salty, with about 35 grams of salt in every kilogram of water. That is as salty as one large spoonful of salt in half a bucket of water!

Saltiest sea

The Dead Sea in Asia is so salty that when its water is turned to vapour by the sun, the salt is left behind in hard white lumps.

vapour – a mist or gas given off when something is heated

Salty sources

Volcanic hot spots on land and on the sea floor add salt to seawater when they release hot gases and molten rock. Rivers wash salt from the land into the seas and oceans.

Grains of salt

Some of the salt we put on our food comes from the sea. Sea-salt is broken up into small pieces so we can sprinkle it on our dinner.

volcanic – *of a volcano or area where molten rock or steam comes to the surface*

Undersea landscape

Hidden under the sea is a world of high mountains, wide plains and deep valleys – a whole landscape as interesting and varied as the one on dry land!

Flattest and deepest

Almost half of the deep ocean floor is a very flat, abyssal plain. Even deeper are the ocean trenches, which plunge 10,000 metres below the surface.

abyssal plain – a large, flat area of land on the sea floor

Mountain top islands

When volcanoes form on the sea floor, they grow into mountains. These can get so tall that they stick out of the sea and make islands.

Black smokers

Deep seawater is usually very cold, but at volcanic spots called black smokers, water three times hotter than boiling gushes through cracks in the sea floor.

trenches – long, narrow valleys, usually formed next to islands or mountains

Tides and waves

Seawater is always moving. It is stirred by the heat of the sun and the cold of the ice at the North and South Poles, pushed by winds, and pulled by the sun and the movement of the moon.

Windy waves

When wind blows over water, it makes waves. Strong winds blowing for a long time make the biggest waves, which can be up to 34 metres high!

coasts – shores, where sea and land meet

Tide out, tide in

The moon pulls water towards it as it goes around the earth, making the seas and oceans bulge away from the coasts. This movement causes tides. Most tides happen twice a day – the sea moves away from the shore (tide out) and back again (tide in).

tide out

tide in

Eating land

In some places waves wash away beaches and cliffs, changing the shape of the coastline in just a few days.

Weather-making sea

The oceans make weather by warming or cooling the air over them, which creates winds and clouds. Ocean currents carry warmth and cold around the planet.

Hooray for rain!
Clouds from the Indian Ocean bring heavy rains to Asia and Africa. Without the rains, crops would not grow.

Hurricane!

Warm, tropical seas sometimes heat the air above them so much it makes wind and rain that build into a giant spinning storm, or hurricane. This type of huge storm can destroy whole towns!

El Niño

Every few years a strange warm current called El Niño sweeps along the west coast of South America, causing extreme weather across the world – devastating storms, droughts, even heavy snow!

currents – *rivers of seawater flowing inside a sea or ocean*

Living history

Life on earth began in the sea, billions of years before there was life on land. Some of those early life forms are alive in the sea today!

First life on earth?

Stromatolites are mounds of millions of tiny creatures. They look just like stromatolites from 3 billion years ago.

Living fossils

The coelacanth fish was known only by fossils millions of years old, until living coelacanths turned up in 1938.

fossils – the remains of ancient animals or plants turned into rock

Unchanged habits

Each year, horseshoe crabs surface from deep water to lay their eggs on sandy beaches, just as they have for 400 million years!

billion – *1,000 million years, written like this: 1,000,000,000*

Fish **rule**

There are more than 20,000 different kinds of fish in all shapes and sizes, and most of them live in the oceans and seas.

Ocean hunters

Big fish, such as this blue shark, are the predators of the sea. Most sharks hunt animals for food, and can swim really fast so they can catch their dinner.

camouflage – a shape, colour or pattern that helps hide an animal

Fish or seaweed?

The leafy sea-dragon has great camouflage. It looks so much like seaweed that it can hide among the plants and not be seen by other fish that might want to eat it.

Safety in numbers

In a shoal of fish there is a greater chance of spotting danger (lots of eyes), and a smaller chance of being eaten (lots of other fish could be eaten instead)!

shoal – a group of one kind of fish

Ocean mammals

Sea mammals are shaped for swimming. They have smooth, streamlined bodies that can slip through the water, and they can hold their breath for a long time when they dive.

Sea flyers

Sea-lions use their webbed front feet to row them along – fast! It is like underwater flying, and it makes catching fish easy!

streamlined – *having a smooth body shape that moves easily through water*

Legless dolphins

Dolphins do not have back legs at all! They swim by beating their tail up and down, and steer with paddle-shaped feet called flippers.

Underwater herbivores

Dugongs also use their tails and flippers for swimming. These large, heavy animals graze on plants called seagrasses, so their other name is 'sea cow'.

herbivores – plant-eating animals

Super sea-birds

Sea-birds are tough! They fly hundreds or thousands of miles every year to find food at sea. They survive storms and rough seas, and still find their way back to land to nest. Phew!

All puffed up

Male frigatebirds puff up their bright red chest like a balloon to impress female birds and find a mate to nest with.

Tiny traveller

The tiny Arctic tern travels 24,000 kilometres every year, from the Arctic Ocean to the Antarctic Ocean.

Long wings

Huge wingspans of up to 3.5 metres carry albatrosses over the stormiest oceans in search of food.

Diving for dinner

Puffins dive for food, using their wings underwater like paddles. They catch small fish to feed to their chicks on land.

wingspans – *distances between wingtips*

Who eats whom?

Ocean life, just like life on land, depends on plants. Plants are eaten by herbivores, and herbivores are eaten by carnivores – this is called a food chain.

Big mouth, short chain!
The whale shark is the world's biggest fish (up to 15 metres long)! Its food chain is very short because it feeds on the smallest animals and plants in the sea – plankton.

carnivores – animals that eat meat

killer whale

eats

porpoise

eats

coá

eats

herring

eats

zoo-plankton

eats

phyto-plankton

Big mouth, long chain

Killer whales need big food – they cannot eat the tiny plankton. There are five links in the food chain between killer whales and the smallest plants in the ocean, phyto-plankton.

zoo-plankton – *a type of plankton that is animal not plant*

Coral reef

In tropical seas, where the water is warm and clear, corals grow like forests of small pink, yellow and white trees. They are full of colourful fish, and many other kinds of life.

Clever clowns!

Little clown fish can hide from danger amongst the stinging tentacles of big anenomes because anenomes never sting their own clown fish!

Super slug

The sea-slug's bright colours are a warning to predators that it has a sting in its orange skin!

Plant-like corals

Corals look like plants, but they are really animals with soft bodies protected by a hard stony skeleton. They are related to anenomes.

tentacles – long, bendy parts of an animal, used for gripping, feeling or moving

Kelp jungles

All over the world, where the sea is cool and the coastline is rocky, there are underwater jungles of huge seaweeds called kelps.

Jungle eaters

Sea-urchins eat kelp and, although they are small, they can munch their way through a forest of seaweed.

... and jungle savers

Luckily, many animals eat sea-urchins.
Seals, dogfish, lobsters and sea-otters,
such as this one floating in a kelp forest
off the west coast of America, love to
snack on the spiky animals.

Frozen feast

Antarctica is the huge frozen land around the South Pole. It looks like an icy desert, but the ocean around it is full of fish, birds, seals and whales.

Penguin crowds
Seven kinds of penguins live in the Antarctic but these adelies are the most common. There can be five million of them in one nesting area!

schools – *groups of whales*

Whale schools

Humpbacked whales, as well as 14 other kinds of whale and dolphin, travel to the Antarctic every summer just to feed.

... and here is what they eat...

Krill! These shrimp-like animals are not big, just 4 centimetres long, but there are a lot of them. A single swarm can cover 45,000 football pitches and weigh 2 million tonnes!

swarm – a large group of small animals

Deep oceans

In the deepest parts of the ocean, it is always cold and completely dark. The pressure of water would squash you flat, yet even here there is life.

Deepest divers

Sperm whales dive 300 to 3,000 metres down to feed on giant squid. They can hold their breath for almost an hour!

Silver camouflage

Hatchet fish stay hidden in deep water by having shiny skin that matches the gleam of the surface far above.

Shine a light

Some animals make
their own light from
chemicals in their
bodies, so they can
find each other in
the dark or scare
off predators.

pressure – *weight of water in the ocean*

Ocean mysteries

Humans have only just begun to explore life in the sea. There is so much we do not know about some of the biggest and most beautiful marine animals.

Giant mystery...

The ocean sun fish or mola mola weighs up to 2,000 kilograms and eats plankton, but that is almost all we know about this huge fish.

marine animals – animals that live in or on the sea

... and mysterious giant

Manta rays can be six
metres across but, like
the mola mola, all we
know about them is that
they swim the oceans
eating plankton.

Bye-bye baby!

Baby turtles hatch on
sandy beaches then
disappear out to sea. We
do not know what they do
next, only that they return
many years later to breed!

Studying the sea

The ocean is not our home – we cannot breathe underwater and we are poor swimmers. However, there are still ways of finding out about the sea.

Follow that seal!

This fur seal has a radio tag attached to its back. It sends signals telling scientists where the seal goes and how deep it dives.

radio tag – a device that sends out invisible signals that travel long distances

Down to the bottom

Tough little submersibles can carry cameras and other equipment to the deepest ocean to find out what goes on there.

Underwater history

Ancient shipwrecks can lie undisturbed on the sea-bed for thousands of years. Modern scuba (breathing) gear helps divers to explore them and discover more about human history.

submersibles – machines that can dive underwater

All fished out

For thousands of years, humans have caught fish to eat. In the past, people used simple nets and sailing boats. But now we use motor boats and huge nylon nets – the fish do not stand a chance.

Useless slaughter

Nets catch anything. Every year, millions of dolphins, turtles, sharks, mola molas and birds die in fishing nets meant to catch something else.

nylon – *tough man-made thread*

Fishing for trouble

People have become too good at fishing. There are now fewer and fewer fish left to catch. Some fish, such as cod, have almost disappeared!

What a waste!

All over the world, people use oceans and
seas as dustbins for all kinds of rubbish
that kills marine life, but it does
not have to be this way.

Stop the spill

If ships carrying oil were
made extra strong, oil
would not spill so easily
when the ships crash.

Safe sewage

Sewage can be made
safe enough to spread
on farmland, not just
dumped into the sea.

Perfect plastic

Plastic rubbish is ugly, and can trap and harm marine animals. This waste can be used again or made so that it breaks down naturally.

sewage – body waste that you flush down the toilet

Tasty sea-slug

You will need
- Block of marzipan
- Plate
- Food colouring and brush
- Coloured sweets

A bitter taste
Sea-slugs are not eaten by anything in the sea – they taste really horrible! However, here is a sea-slug that is tasty to eat.

1

To make the slug's long body, roll the marzipan between your hands into a sausage shape. Then put the shape on to a plate.

2

Many sea-slugs have frills. Use your fingers to press down along the bottom edges of the body to make a frill along each side.

3

Dip your paintbrush into some food colouring and paint the frills. The frills can be any colour. Paint dots of colour down the slug's back.

4

Sea-slugs can be very bright. Decorate the slug's body with coloured sweets. Use two sweets as antennae on the slug's head.

Making waves

Wind-power

Wind blowing across the sea makes waves. The stronger the wind blows, the bigger the waves are. Find out how in this project.

1

You will need
- Large, clear glass bowl
- Water
- Blue food colouring
- Spoon

Fill the bowl half-full with water and add a few drops of blue food colouring. Stir the water to mix.

2 Blow across the surface of the water – this is like wind blowing across the sea. Blow hard and you will see large waves.

Paper-plate fish

Shiny scales

Fish come in all sizes, shapes and colours. Use different colours of shiny paper to make a variety of paper-plate fish.

You will need
- Pencil
- Paper plate
- Scissors
- Glue
- Bottle cap
- 1 silver sheet of paper or foil
- 2 coloured sheets of shiny paper
- Black marker pen

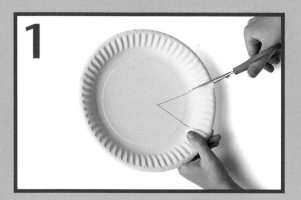

Draw a triangle on the plate and cut it out to make a mouth. Glue the triangle piece on to the body, opposite the mouth, to make a tail.

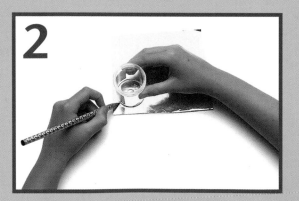

Using a pencil, draw around a round bottle cap and make 30 circles on the sheets of shiny paper.

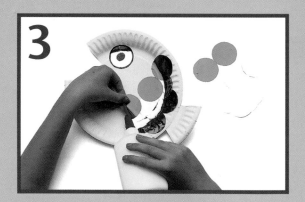

Glue on a silver circle above the mouth and draw a black dot in the centre to make the eye. Then stick the other circles on to the body.

Sandy starfish

Many arms, but no legs!

Most starfish have five arms, but some have more than 50 arms! They use them to move around and to catch prey.

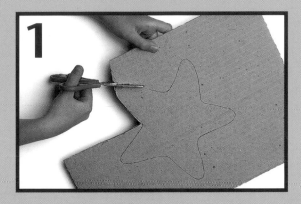

Draw a starfish shape on to the cardboard and cut it out. Copy the starfish shape from this page.

You will need
- Thick cardboard
- Pencil
- Scissors
- Glue and gluebrush
- Teaspoon
- Orange and pink coloured sand

Draw a line about 1 centimetre around the inside of the starfish, following the starfish shape. Spread glue over the inner starfish shape.

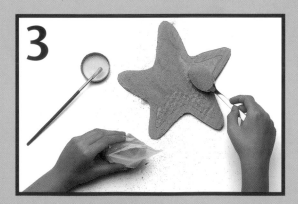

Use the spoon to sprinkle on the orange sand. Press down the sand and leave to dry. Do the same with pink sand on the rim of the starfish.

Jolly jellyfish

Many tentacles

Jellyfish use their tentacles to gather food as they swim. There are over 200 types of jellyfish and some have tentacles that are 30 metres long!

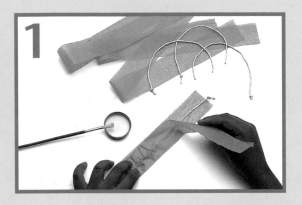

1

Glue each piece of string down the middle of four strips of tissue paper, from top to middle. Fold up the remaining paper to cover the string.

You will need
- Glue and glue brush
- 4 pieces of string, 20cm long
- Green tissue paper cut into 5 strips, 40cm long
- Scissors
- Coloured paper plate
- Sticky tape
- Shiny paper

2

Cut the plate in half. Place each green tissue tentacle on to the back of the plate half and stick each one down with sticky tape.

3

Glue the fifth tissue paper strip along the curve of the plate half. Then cut out circles of shiny paper and decorate the jellyfish body.

Seascape

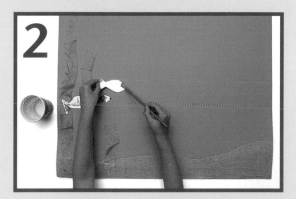

You will need
- Glue and glue brush
- Green tissue paper, cut into strips
- Large piece of hard blue card
- Sand
- Pen or pencil
- Shiny paper
- Scissors

All together
Here, you can create an underwater landscape to show the crafts you have made in this book.

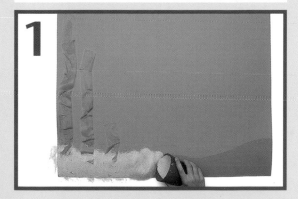

Glue the tissue paper on to the card and spread glue over the bottom of the card. Pour sand over the glue and pat it down.

Draw fish on to the shiny paper. Cut them out and stick them onto the card. You can also add any other sea animals you have made.

Use different coloured paper, foil and sand to make more sea creatures for your seascape.

Index